Merry Christmas
To Jim

From Del & Martha

The Champions'
GUIDE TO
GOLF

The Champions'
GUIDE TO
GOLF

by

GEORGE SULLIVAN

Introduction by
MIKE TURNESA

FLEET PUBLISHING CORPORATION
New York

Acknowledgments

The author wishes to acknowledge, with gratitude, the help of the following in the preparation of this book: Oscar Fraley, Don Weiss, Information Director, and Janet Seagle, United States Golf Association; and Marion H. Miller, Director of Public Relations, Wilson Sporting Goods.

Contents

Introduction

All the average golfer wants is a tip, a hint, a playing secret of some kind that will help him improve his game. This book contains hundreds of them, and each has been professionally tried and proved.

What this book does is describe how the artists do it, and in that way it instructs in the art of golf. It shows how Julius Boros' superb hands guide the wedge shot; how Billy Casper's splendid wrist action enables him to hole putts as well as or better than anyone else in golf. It demonstrates in detail Sam Snead's wonderful one-piece swing.

No phase of golf is overlooked; from tee to green, the champions show how it is done.

It is probably best to read this book with a golf club near at hand. Read what the professional does; then try it. (Some American homes are blessed with ceilings high enough to allow you to swing—at least—a 9 iron.)

Of course, the professional player has other qualities besides his ability to execute his shots in the manner described here. For one thing, he is consistent. When a pro hits, that left arm is always rod-straight. The important word is *always*.

You must be consistent. What you have to do is determine a set of playing characteristics that are right and that suit you. Then stick with these. In any sport—in bowling, in ice hockey, in Australian cricket—individual players must have "stickability," the talent for doing the same thing over and over again.

So it is in golf. Using this book as a guide, plan a playing style for yourself, one that covers every single facet of the game; then stay with it.

Besides consistency, there is another difference between the professional and not so professional player. The pro plans his attack carefully, always playing to his capabilities. Throughout, his game has a tactical aspect.

Your game must be planned in the same way. But remember that your offense has to be mapped out with strict regard for your ability. So first of all, with all the objectivity you can muster, determine your present level as a golfer. Be honest; if your best score last season was 81, that is not your level.

The vast majority of American golfers average in the 90's. If you are in that category, your first step in any improvement program is to admit that fact to yourself. The next step is to seek to take a modest step forward. If you are averaging 92, seek to drop to 87—not 77. Try for pars, not for birdies.

You *can* play better. And, if you allow them, the champions in this handbook will show you how.

Mike Turnesa

The Champions'
GUIDE TO
GOLF

ONE

The Vardon Grip
and Variations

There is not a golf professional alive who will not tell you that the most important factor in all good golf is the grip. Indeed, it is. For it is the grip that couples the hands to the club, and in doing so serves as transfer agent in relaying the strength and the power of the body's coil and uncoil to the club shaft and head.

Everyone agrees the grip is all-important and, moreover, that most all of the mistakes of any poor swing can be traced to a faulty grip. Having the hands and fingers positioned incorrectly, or having hand or finger pressure on the club too loose or too tight, is a sure way to wreck one's game. To most players this knowledge will be about as startling as the news that Sam Snead has never won a national open championship. Yet because it is so important, it is worth repeating.

Well, you ask, if the knowledge of the grip's importance is so universally known, why does the grip continue to be so troublesome; why does it remain the basic cause of almost all of golfing's flubs and fluffs?

Partly the reason is anatomical. The hands are marvelous muscular mechanisms, capable of all variety of movement—more types, in fact, than any other part of the body. They can move forward or back, up or down, or to either side. They can push or pull in any direction. They can work individually or as a perfectly matched team.

For instruments such as these the golf swing is a very simple

1

matter. All the left hand has to do is pull—pull the club into the proper arc of the swing. The right hand has to act more as a guide, though; at the instant of impact, it must exert force equal to that of the left. Of course, the hands in the golf grip work together. They have to in order to relay the optimum in striking speed and force.

This means that the grip not only must unify the hands; it also must have restricting quality, limiting the work of the fingers to the simple yet precise tasks of the swing.

Through the years, and presently, too, golfers have devised a multiplicity of ways of gripping the golf club. It really doesn't matter how you grip the club (though the overlapping grip is much preferred today). What is important is that you bring the club head through the swing with fine, fluid power and in such a way that the club head is at a right angle to the line of flight at the moment of impact. This is what you must accomplish, and it doesn't matter if you have to grip your club as if it were a pickax to accomplish it. If your grip allows you to get rhythmic power in your swing, if it serves to position your club head properly at the point of impact, then your problems in golf will all be very small ones.

A few years ago, *Golf Magazine* surveyed the touring professionals to discover that more than 95 per cent of them used what is called the Vardon grip or its most popular variation, the overlap grip. This grip style is not only in current vogue. It always has been the most popular and, in fact, dates to more than fifty years before the time of Henry Vardon.

What distinguishes the overlap grip from the others styles is that the little finger of the right hand laps over the forefinger of the left.

The left and right hands grip the club in this way: the left hand takes what is called a palm and finger grip. The club is laid diagonally across the palm, extending from the heel of the palm to the root of the forefinger. It is the last three fingers of the left hand that do the work. It is they that provide the lift and the swing, while the thumb and the forefinger merely act as control guides.

The left thumb should extend straight down the shaft. The V formed by the thumb and the forefinger should point to the right shoulder.

The right hand grip is much more a finger grip. Bend the fingers of the right hand. Notice how they form a channel. Simply grip the club by means of this finger channel.

Once the grip is taken, the little finger of your right hand is to be positioned between the forefinger and the middle finger of the left. This is the pure overlap style. The Vardon grip also has an "interlock" variation wherein the little finger is intertwined with the left index finger; and an "unlap" variation, too, whereby the little finger of the right hand is simply positioned close by the left index.)

The thumb of the right hand should curl over the shaft so as to touch the middle finger and the forefinger.

The V formed by the thumb and index finger of the right hand should parallel the left-hand "V." That is, it should point to the right shoulder.

It is the index finger of the right hand, plus the middle finger and the thumb, which should be the controlling factors in the right hand grip. The little finger and the one next to it are simply to guide the swing.

The hands will be coupled together not only by virtue of the fact that the little finger of the right hand laces over the forefinger of the left. But additional unity will be achieved by the way the left thumb fits into the groove of the right palm.

This, then, is the Vardon grip, the overlap as many call it. Palmer, Lema, Venturi, 95 per cent of the professionals use it (with just a slight bit of individual styling of one type or another). If you have never positioned your hands on the club shaft in this manner, the grip will surely feel awkward to you at first. Don't be concerned; this is normal.

It also may feel as if the right hand has been robbed of its power. This is normal, too. This type of grip does serve to give dominance to the left hand. Golf theorists have determined that this characteristic of the grip, mainly by serving to slow the backswing, gives you a better-timed and more rhythmic swing pattern.

Of course, the varieties of the Vardon grip are endless. Just as no two persons' fingers and hands have precisely the same size and shape, so, too, no two persons have the same style of grip. (Vardon himself had unusually long fingers and the overlap suited him fine.) Some players position their hands more on the top of the shaft; some grip the shaft more to the side. What this means is that finding the right grip is to some extent a matter of trial and error.

You have to tinker some. But be careful. Early in his career Tony Lema's attempts to improve his grip came close to being disastrous. Tony burst upon the pro scene in 1958. He won $13,000 that year and pressed Bob Goalby for rookie honors.

Billy Casper shows the overlap grip. (Wilson Sporting Goods)

Despite his success Tony was bothered by a duck hook, and to overcome it he moved both his hands more to the top of the shaft. Now his problems grew. He started pushing the ball—in every direction. His earnings skidded to less than $8,000 in 1959; the following year they were even less.

His poor showing robbed Tony of his confidence. Once, he recalls, he backed off a shot four times. "They were laying odds I'd never hit it," Tony says.

Then, early in 1961, Tony reverted to his old style. The rest is history.

Julius Boros is another player who, in the past, has varied his style but not with any of the dire results that Lema encountered. A few weeks before the 1952 Open, Boros went from an overlap style to an interlock one. (In this, the forefinger of his left hand locked into the little finger of his right.) The style served him well; Boros won the Open that year.

In 1960, he felt the interlock was causing him too much knuckle strain. This was making him fade the ball to the right. So back went Boros to the overlap style. Three years later—still using the overlap— he won the Open again. Take all of this as testimony to Boros' superb natural talents, rather than as an argument that points up the benefits to be derived from changing the grip.

The interlocking style has other adherents. Gene Sarazen was (and is) an interlocker. And so is Claude Harmon. Its most famous practitioner today is Jack Nicklaus.

For anyone whose fingers are on the short and stubby side, the interlocking grip is recommended. In addition to the special quality of lacing the little finger of the right hand between the index and middle finger of the left hand, there is another style characteristic of the interlocking grip. Often the thumb of the left hand is kept outside the palm of the right hand. This helps to prevent wrist lock at the time of impact.

Distinctly different from the Vardon grip and its infinite overlapping, unlapping, and interlocking variations is the baseball grip. As the name suggests, in the baseball style you simply grip the club with the palms of the hands (with the thumbs off the handle) just the way a batter grips a baseball bat or, as Jackie Gleason, who prefers this style, advises, "just the way you'd grab a broom to chase a mouse."

Art Wall and Bob Rosburg are both boosters of the baseball or "ten fingers" grip. The hand control and the free swing the grip is said to give are the principal reasons they like it. Delicate shots are easier with this style, Rosburg claims, "because all the fingers are on the club and so you have a better feel."

The baseball grip is the simplest grip of all. It is exceptionally strong and few things can go wrong with it. Yet its biggest drawback is that it doesn't give the unified and cooperative hand action that the Vardon grip does, and even its adherents admit the right hand can overpower the left as the swing is executed.

In the baseball grip, incidentally, the V's formed by the thumb and forefinger of each hand should point in the same direction as the V's of other and more conventional grips—toward the right shoulder, that is.

Practice the Vardon style. Use one of the variations if one seems to suit you. Almost immediately the grip should present you with a number of advantages.

First of all, it will give you perfect control over the club at every stage. The club will not have the slightest tendency to slip, not even at the highest point of the backswing.

Second, the grip should feel comfortable (though for first practice session or two or three the grip may feel a bit unwieldy).

Third, the hands should work together—and easily. It is a cooperative action; when the pull of one hand increases, the pull of the other decreases.

If your grip gives you control, comfort, and in it the hands work together so that the power of one complements the power of the other, you will soon be wearing out shoe leather making trips to the winner's circle.

One final bit of advice concerning the grip. It has to do with the pressure your hands exert upon the club. This pressure really can't be described in precise terms. However, it can be said that this pressure must be enough so that you maintain control over the club; yet it cannot be so much that the slightest tension is produced in the

Casper overlaps on iron shots, too. (Wilson Sporting Goods)

fingers, wrists, or arms.

Avoid tension as you would a thorny rough. Try this test: hang one arm to your side and clench the hand into a tight fist. Now try to swing the arm. Notice how the tension in the hand stifles the swing. Well, the same thing happens when you allow tension to build as you grip the golf club.

Be particularly on guard against tenseness when you have a long shot to make. The next time you get set to drive a tee shot on a long par 5, look down at your knuckles. If you are clutching the club in a viselike grip, the knuckles will turn white. Swing and you will be lucky to get 175 yards.

Maintaining too little pressure is just as wrong as having too much pressure. It is a common malady for a golfer to show a proper grip at the address and into the backswing; but often, at the top of the backswing, he releases his finger pressure. Then, on the downswing, he seeks to tighten his grip again. The results of such action on the flight of the ball have contributed immensely to the popularity of bowling and skin diving and other non-club sports.

If this grip-ungrip-grip adjustment is done with the right hand, it serves to close the club face just before the moment of impact. A hook is the result.

This habit is most common with the left hand, however. If you regrip the shaft with the left hand at the top of the swing, the grip becomes exclusively a finger grip (instead of a finger-palm combination). This opens the club face. A slice is sure to result.

The moral is: if you are hooking or slicing, look to your grip. In the vast majority of cases, that is where the trouble lies.

Before you take your shot, check your grip. Raise the club; look down at your fingers. The first three knuckles of each hand will be the ones that are visible. The thumbs will be parallel to one another.

Then rest the club head back on the ground and check the V's. They should be pointing to the right shoulder.

Remember to keep the pressure on the club shaft constant, and you're ready to let 'er rip!

TWO

The Professional
One-Piece Swing

"It's a fundamental principle in all athletic games which include the hitting of a ball that the forearm and the handle of the striking implement must at the time of impact be in one and the same straight line, and even in rare cases where this vital rule is apparently violated, it will be found that actually the forearm and the handle of the instrument are in the same straight line as regards the plane of force that is exerted."

P. A. Vaile wrote these words in *Modern Golf,* an instructional handbook published in 1909. Of course the statement is as true now as when the cleek and the niblick were golfers' weapons.

This observation by Mr. Vaile is recorded here because it is so important, for if you can imagine the golf club as simply an extension of your hand and forearm, if you can fix that picture in your mind's eye as you execute your swing, your problems with your swing would be few.

Such an imagining would lead to a natural swing. On the backswing the cocking of the wrists would be less of an intentional maneuver; there would be no abrupt forcing of the hands and arms on the downswing. Throughout, your swing would be smooth and uncomplicated—and that is what it should be.

Professionals average about 250 yards on their drives (though

Jack Nicklaus ("The Big Three," NBC–TV)

Palmer and Nicklaus are consistently longer than that), and every amateur, from the first tee to the eighteenth, seeks to get this kind of distance. There is no part of golf as satisfying as the long, booming hit. Yet there is no trick to attaining distance. Power—club head speed and force—is all that is needed. And power is generated by a smooth and unified blend of hand, body, and leg action from address to follow-through.

The Stance

The good swing begins with the good stance. As you step up to the ball, never fail to make a conscious effort to set the feet and body in precisely the right position.

The feet offer no problem. It's simply a matter of setting them comfortably so their positioning will be wide enough to allow you to turn your body easily. When you use your driver, this means your feet will be about as wide as your shoulders are. Don't go any wider than this. If you do, you will restrict your hip action and thereby stifle your swing.

As you move down from the driver to the deep-faced irons, the feet should move closer together. And when you set yourself for a short wedge shot to the green, say 20 or 30 yards, the feet need not be any more than six or eight inches apart. It's easy to understand why this maneuvering is possible. The arc of the swing is shorter with the deep-faced irons and you don't need as wide a balancing platform as you do with the driver and other woods.

It is not too important how you angle your feet, so long as they give you the maximum amount of stability. Most professional players point the left foot slightly toward the hole (watch Jack Nicklaus; he exaggerates this move); the right foot is angled slightly too, but it is more perpendicular to the line of flight than the left.

It's accepted practice now to hit the wood shots from a closed stance. This means the right foot is drawn back a few inches from the line of flight, an action that permits the hips to turn easily and as much as is required.

The long irons are struck from a square stance (both feet parallel to the line of flight), and the shorter irons are hit from an open stance (the left foot drawn back from the intended line of flight). Of course, the stance with the wedge is more open than any of the others.

Pick the feet positioning that suits your shot. Dig in. Bend your knees somewhat; this will help you to relax.

Now the hips—be careful here. The hips have to be positioned in such a way they can turn with ease, in combination with the shoulders. The body is so constructed that it's very simple to turn the shoulders without turning the hips, but in golf, if you do this (and there is a tendency to), your swing will be a disaster.

When you take your stance, it's just as if you were getting in position to sit on a high stool. Granted, it's awkward, but repetition will make it feel natural for you.

Sam Snead likes to tell about a match with President Eisenhower, when Ike, having trouble with his swing, asked Snead for advice.

"Well, er, Mr. President," Sam drawled. "Why don't you try sticking your, er, fanny out a little more?"

The advice worked, Sam says. The General played in fine style for the rest of the match. Let it be a lesson to you. A tucked in derriere is sure to cramp your swing.

Of course, none of this is meant to imply you should be in a full bend or a crouch as you prepare to hit. Indeed you should not.

Your position relative to the ball should prevent any tendency to crouch. When you position the club face in back of the ball, you should be standing upright (but not straight up). Your arms should hang loosely—naturally—from the shoulders. Your weight should be evenly distributed over both feet.

Invariably golfers get two pieces of advice about the position of the head. "Keep your head still," says one. "Keep your head down," says another. The first admonition is a valid one. The second is, too, but with some reservations.

And as anyone who has played the least bit of golf can attest, "Keep your eyes on the ball" is yet a third often-voiced caution. Let it be said at once that this warning is somewhat misleading.

You must keep your head still when you swing. You must! When the club face comes through to strike the ball your head must be in precisely the same position it was at the address. It cannot move a millimeter.

If you move your head to the right you will slice. If you move it to the left you will hook. Raise your head and you raise the clubhead; you will top the ball. Lower your head and you lower the clubhead; you will hit behind the ball.

"Keeping your eyes on the ball" will not solve any of these problems for you. You can glue your eyes to the ball and still move your head. In fact, if you're hitting from the first tee, you can probably walk to the club house without taking your eyes from the ball. It's not the eyes that cause trouble; it's the head. Anchor it in place, then hold it there.

Last, let's consider the advice, "Keep the head down." This can be followed only if you take it as a warning not to turn or move your

head during the swing. But don't make the mistake of tucking your chin to your chest when you hear these words. Some golfers do. Such an action can serve to put the ball and the clubhead out of proper focus for you.

After the impact, the head can move; it can come up. Allow the natural movement of the body to turn the head to the left.

You may have noticed that most of the professional players assume a stance position in more or less the manner described above. Arnold Palmer does. When setting himself to drive the ball, he uses a closed stance—the right foot drawn back an inch or two from the intended line of flight of the ball. His feet are spread to shoulder width. He shows one other characteristic that may be helpful to you. As he addresses the ball, he holds his arms so the elbows are slightly bent. This diminishes any feeling of tension in his arms.

Where should the ball be placed in the stance? This depends of course on the club you're using.

On drives, the ball should be on a line with the left heel. When you are using fairway woods, the ball should be an inch or so closer to the right foot. For the irons, the ball is about midway between the feet. Last, for the pitching wedge, the ball should be played off the heel of the right foot.

In the succession of moves from stance to swing, don't overlook the "waggle," the slight movement of the clubhead at the ball that, in many cases, appears as a kind of edited version of the swing itself. In producing the brief motion of the waggle, you serve to reduce the tension in your body that may have built during the time it took you to fix your stance.

Be careful with the waggle. Its tempo helps to set the style and the pace of the swing. "As ye waggle so shall ye swing," say the Scots.

The Backswing

The backswing, the slow arcing of the club head to a point above the level of the right shoulder—and the swing throughout, for that matter—should be kept as simple as possible.

Take the club head back smoothly and deliberately, like an archer drawing a bow. Remember, this is the most critical phase of the entire swing.

In initiating the backswing, no wrist action is necessary. Here, as at the point of impact, "the forearm and the handle of the instrument must . . . be one and the same." It's almost as if you were sliding the club to the right, keeping it parallel to the ground all the way.

What leads the swing? Is it the hands? The shoulders? The hips? There are theories of the golf swing that will support each of these.

But don't be concerned about this point. If you asked a young boy to skim a stone across a lake, he wouldn't be concerned with how he was going to do it. He wouldn't stop to think when he would have to cock his wrist, nor how much backswing he should use. He would simply take the stone and fire it.

Golfing theories and theorists can clutter your mind terribly. Like the boy tossing the stone across the lake, be natural. Let the club head, hands, and shoulders move as a unit.

Some golf instructors say the backswing should begin off what is termed a "forward press." This is the phrase used to describe the forward motion of the hands, arms, and club face at the address; it's part of the waggle. But the club head, instead of striking the ball, recoils from it, and this recoil is what intiates the backswing. This action sometimes helps in getting rhythm into the swing, but it's certainly not a necessity.

When the hands have moved past the right knee, break the wrists. What happens is really more of a side bend than a break, with the right wrist leading the action. The club face of course remains square to the line of flight.

Slowly, your hands move to the top of the swing, the cocking (or bending) of the wrists increases. The club face remains square.

Now you have hit the top of your swing. It is difficult to say just where or when your turn will end. But there are two bits of advice you can follow here. First of all, do not let the turn go so far that you lose control of the club. Your grip must have the same firmness at the apex of the swing as it had at the address.

"Control of the hands is the Number One element in the golf swing, and it always will be," Jerry Barber, 1961 Player of the Year and P.G.A. Champion, told an annual meeting of two hundred golf pros. Really, there is no advice that is better. Loosen the grip one iota and you are certain to destroy the rhythm and fluid action of the swing.

Second of all, you must not bend the left arm. Bend the right, of course—you will have to in order to break your wrists, but never the left.

Watch the professionals. Every one of them will carry the left arm rod-straight (but never tense) throughout the swing.

The feet must be spread to shoulder width. Dave Marr gets set to hit. (CBS Golf Classic)

You must keep your head still when you swing. (Brunswick Corporation)

So swing back as far as you can—but not so far that there is even the slightest weakening of your grip; and not so far that there is the slightest break in your left arm.

At the top of your swing, your weight has shifted to your right foot. The foot and leg are positioned almost as they were at the address. Guard against the slightest weakening; the leg, the foot should offer really solid support in order to assure proper balance. Any loss of balance diminishes the distance you get.

The Downswing

What happens after the backswing has reached its zenith is a cause of mighty controversy among golf instructors. And if you ask ten professional players how the downswing is initiated, you are very likely to get ten different answers.

It's the left hip that leads the action, says one school; the hands and the arms do it, says another. "Rotate your shoulders first," says one very popular theory. Whole books have been written on the contention that it's "the body pivot launched by the feet" that initiates the downswing.

Some instructors point out there should be a definite pause at the top of the swing. Every action connected to the backswing comes to a dead stop, they say. There is a split-second hesitation; then everything shifts into reverse.

Whether there is an observable pause at the swing's apex is a point that can be debated. But if you are conscious of such a pause and of the reverse to forward shift in gears, it is a fairly safe bet that you are swinging at the ball in much the same way Jack Nicklaus would play third base.

Do not be concerned with such technical triflings. You have too much of importance on which to concentrate. You have to be concerned with keeping your head still; you have to concentrate on keeping your grip firm; you have to remember not to break your left elbow. These have to be uppermost in your mind. If you are worried about such things as "the body pivot launched by the feet," it is almost certain that you will be a strayer.

If your backswing is right, the downward swing of the club will follow naturally. In fact, by the time the club head reaches the apex

of the swing, the downswing has already begun. They flow, one to the other.

When your hands reach a point in the backswing where there is danger of losing control of the club, they recoil into a reverse direction. But the hips anticipate this recoil; they turn toward the left. The left hip leads the way; the hands, arms, and club follow. As this takes place, the body weight shifts from the right foot to the left.

The left hip lead will happen by itself. There is no need to make a conscious effort to turn or swing the hip.

A word of warning here. As the downswing begins, there is a tendency to relax the grip. (When the fingers flex on the club handle, some pros call this "playing the piccolo.") Beware; don't let up on the control of the club for a single instant.

Now the arms and club are coming through to hit the ball. The wrists remain fully cocked.

Here is where the pro players are separated from those who are not so pro. The professional is able to delay the uncocking of the wrists until the very last split second before impact. Some, like powerful Mike Souchak, have the wrists cocked as late as when the hands are passing the hips. The club is nearly vertical.

What this means is that in the brief span of the swing arc left to him, Souchak must move the club head ten to twelve times as much as he will move his hands. This gives the club head tremendous acceleration. Did you ever wonder why professional players get so much more distance than you do? This delayed uncocking of the wrists which generates the great club head speed in the final stages of the swing is the prime reason.

A brief look at the physics of it shows why this is true. Force equals mass times acceleration. The player can do little about mass—the size and density of the club head. Mike Souchak's club head is probably very much like your own. The only other variable is acceleration or velocity. And when acceleration is increased, force—or what is called exertion of power—is multiplied in proportion. Increased "exertion of power" is a fitting way to explain 300-yard drives.

The delayed wrist action is not precisely simple to execute. (Tony Lema is one who is a master at the technique. Notice the photo of Tony on page 30.) It takes no small amount of hand and wrist and arm strength. It is usual for the pros to have forearms with muscles that bulge like those of a blacksmith. That is one reason they can snap the club as they do.

Another reason has to do with natural ability. The delayed wrist uncocking requires perfect timing, and usually this is not an acquired trait.

You will have to decide yourself just how long you can delay the wrist snap when you swing through the ball. It depends on your physical prowess, your natural ability, and your experience in the sport, too.

When the wrists uncock, the club head whips through the ball. In this way, the player submits to Mr. Vaile's premise, expressed in the opening paragraph, that the "forearm and the handle of the striking implement must, at the time of impact, be in one and the same straight line."

The stroke now blends into the follow-through. Here, as some players describe it, they "pronate" (to make prone) their wrists and turn them over, so that the back of the left hand is parallel to the ground. Again, there need not be any conscious effort on your part to accomplish this. In fact, if you don't pronate and turn, it will be awkward for you—even difficult—to keep a firm grasp on the club shaft.

The momentum of the swing will carry the hands, wrists, arms, shoulders, and hips to a full finish. This natural flow of action will—at the end—lift the right heel from the ground. The head will turn to follow the ball. An observer doesn't have to look down the fairway to see if you have hit a good shot. Your finishing position will tell the story. If it's a picture-book type, so is your drive.

Throughout, the swing has to be timed to perfection. What differentiates a pro's swing from an amateur's is the manner of timing. The amateur has a tendency to rush into the downswing from the apex. Accelerative force generated at this stage is wasted.

But the professional holds back on the power surge until the point of impact. When he wants power, and when he needs it, he has it. The delayed uncocking of the wrist does the trick.

Of course, no two professional players swing in the same way. Each features certain characteristics of style and these serve to give added power or increased accuracy or both. Some of these may be helpful to you.

There are some theorists on the tour who prefer the upright swing, one where the club ascends almost straight up into the backswing and then straight down. Opposed to this is the "flat" swing, where the club is swung in an arc that is more parallel to the ground, something like the batter's swing in baseball.

Sam Snead has an upright swing; Hogan's swing is flat. The upright swing, incidentally, is the one currently in vogue among the touring professionals, and many observers claim that it is one of the main reasons golfers get more distance today than ever before. Yet the flat swing has served Doug Ford well through the years, and

Arnold Palmer's swing tends toward the flat side, too.

It's probably best not to make an effort to be either flat or upright in style. Simply follow the guideposts for the swing set down in the earlier paragraphs of this chapter. The particularities will come naturally.

Jack Nicklaus has very much of an upright swing; you've probably noticed. Another feature of Nicklaus' swing that gets him distance is his characteristic of moving his right elbow away from his right side during the middle and latter stages of his backswing. (Be wary about trying this; it can quickly throw your timing out of kilter.) With the right elbow so positioned, Jack is able to get a much wider swing arc than normal and hence more power.

Some players—Chi Chi Rodriguez is a prime example—utilize their legs to a greater degree than is implied in the instruction hints set down here. As Rodriguez moves the club head into the backswing, he cocks his right leg toward the ball—to the *right*, that is. This enables him to get the clubhead around faster on the downswing. For Rodriquez it works; his drives are often of the "ooh and aah" type.

No matter what nuances of style might be included in your swing, over-all it should include these characteristics:

—a solid yet comfortable stance.
—a determination to keep the head still.
—a firm grip throughout.
—a straight left arm.
—smooth, deliberate action in the backswing; the delayed wrist snap in the downswing.

Fortunately you can practice golf's swing at any time of year in your backyard or in your living room. Remember—it's a "one-piece swing," a thing of fluid rhythm from start to finish. That's the dominating characteristic you should strive for.

A full follow-through is a must. (CBS Golf Classic) →

THREE

The Driver

"We drive for fun and putt for money," the pros are supposed to proclaim. They don't. The statement is a fairly inaccurate one.

Of course, to score well in golf, putting is the most important ability you can have. Yet the talent to drive runs it a close second—a very, very close second.

I think the main reason the shot off the tee has such great value is purely psychological. If you can drive 225 yards straight down a fairway (and past your playing partners), it makes you feel good. It puts zing into your entire game; it gives you a wonderful confidence. The next shot is likely to be a good one, and then the next and the next.

This is not meant to imply that the distance drive, the particularly long one, that is, is the one you should pursue on every shot. It must be said at once that accuracy is more important than distance.

Jack Nicklaus is generally considered the best of the pros off the tee today. His swing is built along classic lines; he boasts a full turn, a huge and sweeping club head arc. But what few observers stop to realize is that Nicklaus is as accurate as he is long, and that great success is owing to his accuracy more than his ability to powder the ball 300 yards down the fairway.

Television's presentation of golf competition gives you a remark-

25

able opportunity to learn how the pros use their ability to be accurate. On TV, before the play of each hole, an artist's sketch or aeriel photograph of the hole from tee to green is shown. What you should do is relate that sketch to how the pro plays the hole.

Notice where they tee the ball, and how they place the tee shot in an area that opens up the green for an easy approach. (Don't be discouraged if you're not able to hit your target on every drive. Not even the best players do; notice the chart on page 34.)

Pros never fail to put their drives into a very precise area. Ben Hogan has been known to drive into the rough so that his second shot would be open to the green.

Also take note of how the pro will plan his tee shot so as to avoid trouble. If there is rough or bunkers strewn along the left side of the fairway, the pro will tee his ball on that side and drive to the opposite. I once saw Sam Snead, in an effort to avoid trouble on the left, position his tee shot in such a way that the tee marker was between Sam and the ball as he addressed it. The marker didn't faze Sam and neither did the rough on the left; he got an easy par.

Snead, of course, has been acclaimed as being the "perfect model" for any golfer who is seeking to improve his technique with the driver. His swing is truly magnificent, and it bears many of the fundamental characteristics yours should have.

His stance is comfortable and relaxed. He takes the club head back smoothly, deliberately. Notice how his right arm stays straight throughout. Notice how the head hardly moves.

Snead's body uncoils superbly. There is not the slightest hint of a hurried movement. The wrists remain cocked until the hands pass the waist; then the club head is whipped through the ball.

Snead testifies that most of the speed of his swing is generated when the club head is from three to three and one half feet from the ball. Another Snead characteristic, well to note, is that his hands and wrists return to the same position at the point of impact as they held at the address of the ball. This is really the only position for the hands if the club face is to meet the ball squarely.

A full turn, exceptional balance, and masterful timing—all are Ben Hogan traits. (Shell's Wonderful World of Golf") →

Sam Snead has been acclaimed as the "perfect model" for any golfer seeking to improve his technique with the driver. He takes the club head back smoothly, deliberately. The right arm is straight throughout. The head hardly moves. On the downswing his wrists remain cocked until his hands are past his waist. (Wilson Sporting Goods)

← *Sam Snead has a full hip turn, and a full and high follow-through. (Wilson Sporting Goods)*

Notice that Snead likes to play his drives off his left heel; in fact, he plays all his woods that way—that is, up to the number 4 wood wherein he moves the ball slightly back toward center. Snead's stance is a slightly open one, by the way.

Of course, on his drive, it is the full shoulder turn which is Snead's most noted trademark. Snead is able to coil to such an extent that at the top of his backswing the club passes the horizontal. This bit of business gives him a tremendous arc and rates as the major factor for the great club head speed "The Slammer" is able to generate.

Be a bit wary about trying this the next time you step up on the tee, however. When the club passes the horizontal on the backswing, there is a tendency to "lose" the club. The left hand has difficulty maintaining its proper grip pressure at the top and so, on the downswing, there is a tendency to open the club face. A slice, a miserable banana ball, is the result. But if you are able to get that full shoulder turn into your swing like Samuel Jackson Snead and still maintain left-hand control over the club, watch out, you'll be moving up in class—way up, in fact.

Some players, of course, can't turn like Snead; they're restricted by a lack of muscular flexibility.

To develop your own backswing, and in the right amount, there are a couple of general rules you can follow. Swing the club back as far as you can without losing control of it. Of course, don't turn or pivot so much that you are forced to move your head—even the least bit.

Among the latterday professionals, the drives of Jack Nicklaus probably draw more attention than anyone else's. When he addresses the ball Jack turns his left foot toward the target more than is usual. He feels that when he comes through the ball this position-

Nicklaus   **300**

Casper   Furgol   Hiskey   Campbell   Brewer   **280**

Baxter   Charles   Palmer   Harris   Harney
Howell   Sikes   Collins   Dill
Nieporte   Hebert   Lema   Fairfield   Jacobs

Bayer   Cupit   Gabal   Ogden   Boies
Nichols   January   Greenbaum   Rosburg   Geiberger
Sifford   Snead   **260**

Rudolph   Love
Floyd   Crampton   Venturi   Scodeller
Riegel   Beck   Panasiuk   Finsterwald   Littler
Wysong   Farquhar

Sanders   Archer
Harbert   **240**

Bradley

Clark
Player   **220**

Pros don't always drive with unerring accuracy. Here is how players spotted their shots on the 6th hole of the fourth round of the 1964 National Open at Congressional Country Club, Washington, D.C. (Ken Venturi was the eventual winner.) Information for this chart was gathered by Jack Reddy, Golf Analyst, U.S.G.A.

ing of the left foot serves to give him a fuller and easier turn. The follow-through isn't restricted in the least.

Jack's legs are a real key in the tremendous distance he gets with his drives. When he coils into the backswing, he seems to store up power in his right leg. On the downswing—by means of a slight push-off—this power is released. It is not only on his drives that you can notice that characteristic; it is part and parcel of every one of Nicklaus' distance shots.

Ben Hogan, always respected for his skill with the driver, is another professional who can boast superb leg action. And, like Snead, he has a long backswing, and he brings the club head through the ball on a flatter than normal trajectory.

Of course, Hogan's swing reflects a few other important characteristics, none of which are truly simple to develop. He has a full turn, exceptional balance, and masterful timing.

The biggest hitter in golf today is George Bayer, a ten-year veteran of the pro tour. Hold a driving contest and Bayer will win it. Why? The answer is easy.

Bayer stands six foot five; he weighs 240. With such proportions going for him, it's possible for Bayer to create a greater swing arc than almost anyone else, and that is precisely what he does. He gets the very most from his arc potential by means of a fine full pivot. And it goes without saying that Bayer is well balanced in his swing, and perfectly timed.

In Sydney, Australia, Bayer once hit a drive that traveled almost 500 yards, but he points out that, "the wind was with me, and the fairway was like concrete." Anyone for tennis?

Of course, not Bayer nor any other professional on the tour is able to get straight down the middle on every single drive. Just look at the chart on page 34. A typical tournament hole, it shows the tremendous variation in the way the pros place their drives.

Like Christmas or a summer shower, one's aptitude for driving comes and goes. Some days your drives will hook; some days you will slice.

With most of these faults, what you have to do is learn to live with them. Don't make the mistake of attempting a major overhaul in your game in the midst of a round. If a sudden hook develops, first try simple tinkering to correct things. Check your grip or the ball position at the time of address. If corrections here fail to remedy the situation, what you should do is compensate for the hook or fade. Tomorrow it may be gone.

Of course, if you slip out of the groove altogether, that's another matter. The best thing you can do is slow down. Forget about 200 yards; start trying for 160 or 170.

Bring the clubhead back with studied slowness. Feel every part of the swing—the wrist cock, the intitation of the downswing; the straightness in the left arm, the follow-through—everything. Gradually you may work yourself out of trouble. But of course the best place to iron out problems, large or small, is on the practice tee.

The tee shot also brings up the question of *how* to tee the ball. "Tee the ball more high than low," is the general advice to follow. And of course always tee at a level spot.

When you are driving against the wind, tee low. This will help to keep the ball close to the ground. Naturally, when driving downwind, tee high.

When it comes time for you to pick out a new set of clubs, the selection of the driver should get more consideration than any other club—except the putter, of course.

First of all, examine the driver to see if it is of proper length. Test the club this way: hold the shaft upright with the sole of the club head flat to the ground. Place your hands on the grip just as if you were going to swing the club, remembering all the while to keep the sole perfectly flat.

If your hands are out in front of you, if your back is just slightly bent; and if, over-all, your stance is well balanced and feels natural, then the club is right for you.

If, however, this test brings you to a stance wherein you are upright or close to it and your hands are about at your waist, then you know the club is too long for you. And if this posturing brings you to a stance where you have to bend over uncomfortably, then the club obviously is too short.

Second, you should pick out a driver with the right amount of resiliency, or whip as it is called. The shaft of your driver shouldn't be stiff and unyielding. Instead it should have a springlike quality and this should be especially noticable from the top of the backswing to the point of impact.

If the whip exists in the right relationship to your swing, it can give you added power and added distance. If you have a powerful swing featuring lots of wrist action, you probably give the shaft enough whip on your own. Therefore your clubs don't need much resiliency built into them. Of course, the converse is true; if you have a slow steady swing, you may be able to benefit from whippy shafts.

A third factor to be considered when buying clubs is the weight of the club. Clubs should be light enough so you can swing easily and get a full amount of wrist action. But they should not be so light in weight that you lose control of them. A happy medium has to be found.

It is always good practice to get the advice of a professional when buying clubs. And, if you can, seek counsel from a pro who knows your game.

There is a striking similarity in Sarazen's stance as he addresses the ball . . . and as he brings the club head through the swing. (Shell's "Wonderful World of Golf.")

Playing Golf, 1810.

FOUR

The Fairway
Woods

"Wood clubs are commonly employed to propel the ball from where it lies in free and open ground, where there is a good chance of getting it well away, and little fear of breakage." So wrote Robert Forgan in *The Golfer's Handbook* in 1885.

And so it is today (though the fear of breakage may be much less than it was in Mr. Forgan's time.) However, despite the fact that the proper play of almost every hole decrees the use of a fairway wood and does, too, present the chance of getting the ball "well away," the average golfer shies from using his woods on the fairway.

Yet no one denies the importance of these clubs. They make pars possible on long par four holes; they set up birdies on par fives.

Why, then, if it is so important, does the average golfer avoid the fairway woods? The answer to that is easy: because of a consistent lack of success with them. If there is the slightest flaw in your swing, it will come to light when you stroke a wood from the fairway. Your swing here *must* be precise.

You can take a tip from Mike Souchak here. On his wood shots he chokes up just a little bit on his grip. This gives him a shorter swing (and costs him 10 to 15 yards in distance), but it makes him much surer of an accurate swing and a full hit.

Aside from this adjustment, the basic swing on the fairway woods should be about the same as on all other clubs. The stance is more open than it is on a drive—about square, in fact. And at address, your weight should be slightly on your left foot, your hands a bit in front of the ball.

Where should the ball be placed? Generally, about an inch past the left heel.

On his fairway woods, Arnold Palmer places the ball in a fashion typical of most professionals. If he wants more than normal loft, he plays more forward. If he wants to keep the ball low, he plays the ball back toward the center of his stance.

Another reason the average player has difficulty with his fairway woods is that when he uses them, he presses for all the distance he can get. He heaves his body into the ball. Distance is important, of course, but not to the degree that it should influence your swing in the slightest.

The distance you have to go should not even be the determining factor in the selection of wood to use. Aside from the driver, the woods are numbered 2, 3, and 4, with the number designating the slope of the hitting face. The number 4 wood, with its greater slope, is a much easier club to use than the 3 or the 2.

The point is this: If the distance to the green is 250 yards, and you feel certain you can get 200 yards with your number 3 wood, use it. Don't go to the 2 if you have the slightest concern about your lie. And if the lie for your 3 wood shot bothers you, use your 4 wood— and no matter the distance! Never gamble with a wood.

Many professionals will recommend a 5 wood for the average golfer. It is the best club for achieving distance from tight lies.

Among the current touring pros, Bobby Nichols has one of the soundest swings when it comes to the fairway woods. He is powerful; he is accurate.

Nichols takes the club back slowly, and both his arms remain fully extended until the club is waist high. His left shoulder turns down and under his chin. He gets a full hip turn, too, though throughout

Snead's right hand climbs over the shaft as the club head comes through. (Shell's "Wonderful World of Golf") →

he keeps his heels to the ground.

The club head is still moving back as his hips and knees begin to drive forward, so at the time of impact the left hip and side have cleared easily. The wrists are cocked until the club head passes the right knee. When they release, the hands come through at terrific speed.

All professional players boast superb rhythm and perfect balance throughout. There is real power but never the slightest sense of body heave or strain.

The club should hit the ball a descending blow. If the ball is positioned properly—an inch or two off the left foot—this won't be too difficult a task.

As the club head comes through, the leading edge of the sole of the club head should touch the turf at the same instant the club face touches the ball. Attaining this precision is another factor that makes the shot with the fairway wood a difficult one.

On the follow-through, the right arm is almost straight. The wrists pronate and the right one climbs over the shaft.

On any single round of golf, the lies you get on the fairway will differ widely. And each differentiation requires an adjustment in your address. Incidentally, on lies that vary at all from the perfect, it is best to use a 3 or 4 wood. Save the 2 wood for the flawless lies on level stretches of fairway.

On an uphill lie, one where the left foot is tiered higher than the right, play the ball a bit more toward your right foot. This is to compensate for the fact that the bottom of the arc of your swing will occur at a later point in your swing. (This positioning may give the ball a higher trajectory than is normal for the swing and thereby cut down a bit on the distance you hope to get.)

It will feel awkward but you must keep your body weight concentrated on your left side throughout the swing. Fight off any tendency to sway. Simply bring the club back slowly and smoothly, letting it follow the contour of the slope.

The downhill lie—where the right foot is higher than the left—forces you to make other adjustments. Here the ball should be played toward the left heel. And because of the slope of the ground (upward from where you're standing), you have to pick up the club

Chi Chi Rodriguez gets a full turn on a fairway wood shot. (CBS Golf Classic)

head quickly so it won't strike the turf in the backswing. This unnatural condition makes the shot a difficult one to execute correctly.

Two other types of lies are troublesome. One is where the ball rests downhill from (or below) the point where you take your stance; the other is where the ball lies uphill from (or above) you.

On the first of these—when the ball is below the feet—hold the club at the end of the shaft. Square the stance. And keep in mind that this shot is very likely to slice, so be ready for it.

When the ball is above you at the address, choke up on the club. Watch out; this shot will hook.

If you play early-morning golf, inevitably you will find yourself confronted by yet another troublesome wood shot, hitting the wood from wet or dewy grass. The average golfer should limit himself to the use of the 4 wood here, and attempt to pluck the ball cleanly from the turf when he swings. When wetness prevails and you are using a fairway wood, you have much less margin for error than under normal conditions. Take your time; be very careful.

Playing a wood from the sand of a fairway bunker is often a complete disaster. This is because, in trying to recover, the average golfer attempts to blast the ball all the way to the green. Distance shouldn't be your primary goal in these cases.

What you must do is bring the club head through the swing so it hits the ball squarely. Skim the flat sole of the club head over the sand as it meets the ball. That way you *will* get distance.

It doesn't really matter too much what type of fairway wood confronts the average golfer; he makes the same mistake on every one of them. He presses for distance; he presses for loft. To drive the ball, and to drive it far and high in the air, is alone a matter of letting the club do the work it was designed to do.

With the fairway wood, what you have to do is concentrate on your swing. Keep it smooth; keep it well timed. Simply let the club perform for you. You'll get your distance—and in time you'll come to have professional-like confidence and trust in the fairway woods.

Sarazen's wrist cock and uncock deliver the tremendous power of the body's uncoil. Notice how his head remains motionless. (Shell's "Wonderful World of Golf") →

FIVE

The Irons

Under present-day golfing regulations, your golf bag can contain no more than 14 clubs. Usually this means it will have three woods—a driver, a 2 wood and 3 *or* a 4 wood. It will have a putter, a sand wedge, a pitching wedge, and eight irons, numbers 2 through 9.

Most of the professionals equip themselves in this fashion, although some of them, Sam Snead for one, trade off the 3 or 4 wood for a 1 iron.

The point is this. The irons are the most-used of any category of clubs. So you just have to be proficient with them. And the chances are very good that if you are swinging smoothly and accurately with your irons, you will be with your other clubs too.

More often than not, it is the iron shot that determines whether your score on a hole is good, poor, or fair. It's the long iron from the fairway or perhaps the short punch with the 5 that is the most important shot in setting up your par. Hit this shot like an expert and you'll be putting for a birdie; hit it in nonexpert fashion and your score is certain to balloon.

← *Arnold Palmer ("The Big Three," NBC–TV)*

Irons, of course, are classified according to their range, and as follows:

Club number	Maximum distance	Minimum distance	Average
	Long irons		
1	220	190	200
2	200	170	185
3	190	160	175
	Middle irons		
4	180	150	165
5	170	140	155
6	160	130	145
	Short irons		
7	150	120	135
8	140	110	125
9	130	100	115

The professional player knows almost to the last inch the distance he can achieve with any given iron. So, too, you must know what every club will do for you. Not only must you know the distance you can achieve with each, you must also know how much loft you are going to get. The chart above, keep in mind, is to serve you only as a general guide.

The important thing to remember about iron play itself is that every shot, no matter what club is used, has to be executed with the same type of swing. In other words, use the same easy natural swing on the 2 iron as you do when you are hitting an 8 or a 9. If you notice, the pros always do. It's a distinguishing trademark of their game.

Of course, one thing that does change on every iron shot is the positioning of the ball. On the 5 iron, the ball should be about midway between the feet. Low-numbered clubs are hit more off the left foot. (Long-hitting George Bayer positions the ball for his 1 iron shot in precisely the same way as for his drive); high-numbered balls are to be hit from a position near the right foot. In fact the 9 iron and the wedge should be struck from a position nearby the right heel.

Delayed wrist action gives Tony Lema his great power. (CBS Golf Classic)

On this iron shot, Billy Maxwell's swing is a completely natural one. His backswing isn't high, yet he gets a full shoulder turn. His hands lead the club on the

...ownswing; there is a full wrist cock. The club head strikes the ball with a descending blow. (Wilson Sporting Goods)

Maxwell hits the turf and the ball at the same time; notice the divot. The left

side leads the shot into a high follow-through. (Wilson Sporting Goods)

The reason for this is evident. As Mr. Vaile explains it, "You must be careful to stand easily and naturally and at such a distance from your ball that your club shall be touching when soled from heel to toe along the ground, and so that when you make your stroke, it will pass in this manner over the spot where the ball lay." In other words, positioning the ball in the manner described in the above paragraph, aids in having the ball struck at the very bottom of the swing arc.

Your grip on your iron shots should have more firmness than is normal—normal for woods, that is. This is because there is more of a tendency for an iron club to turn in your hand than there is for a wood.

If you have a chance, watch Billy Maxwell, the sandy-haired Dallas professional, when he plays his irons. Notice how he keeps both hands slightly ahead of the club head. All professionals show this trait in iron plays. This assures maximum opportunity of hitting the ball first, and then the turf, rather than scuffing into the turf before striking the ball.

As Maxwell demonstrates, the stance on iron shots is generally a square one. On the 8 and 9 iron, and on pitch shots, the stance is more open, that is, the right foot is placed forward of the left.

Non-professional players usually have great difficulty with the long irons—the 1, 2, and 3 irons. No one denies that these are probably the hardest clubs in the bag to play. Yet, on the other hand, no one denies the great usefulness of these clubs. They are used whenever your lie is a poor one and a wood can't be played, yet they get much the same distance as from your woods.

George Bayer is a standout player with the long irons—particularly the 1 iron. So is Arnold Palmer. Palmer, in fact, credits his 2 iron with winning him important tournaments. The American Golf Classic at Firestone in 1962 is an example. On the long and tough par 3's at Firestone—the 230-yard 5th, the 225-yard 7th, the 180-yard-12th and 230-yard 15th—Palmer used his 2 iron almost exclusively. He was able to play these holes in three under par.

The problems that the average golfer has with the long irons stem from two major fears. First, he is afraid that he is not going to get the distance he needs, so he presses on his shot. He will overpower his swing with his shoulders. This, of course, is a grievous mistake.

The high finish is a mark of the solid swing. Bobby Nichols demonstrates. (CBS Golf Classic)

Notice that the long irons are longer shafted than the other clubs, and this distinction, if the club is swung smoothly and with a full pivot, will serve to get the added distance needed. In other words, let the club do the work, the work it was specifically designed for.

The average golfer also fears he will not be able to get the loft he wants or needs when he strikes an iron shot. In an effort to get his loft, he lifts up his body as he takes his swing. The result is a topped

After impact, Mason Rudolph continues through the ball . . . and into a high follow-through. (CBS Golf Classic)

ball or an arcing slice. The pro player, on the other hand, looks and is firmly rooted to the ground when he makes an iron shot.

A key factor on the long irons is the backswing. How long should it be? This is difficult to answer. Each player has to work the problem out for himself.

Arnold Palmer, when he swings a long iron, gets a full shoulder turn into the shot. At the top of his swing his back is facing the hole. Naturally, when he unwinds, he generates tremendous power.

But be a bit wary if you seek to emulate Mr. Palmer or someone like him. Turning this far could cause you to lose control of the club. The general rule to follow is: turn on the long iron shot as far as you can without losing control of your grip or bending your left arm.

The wrists should remain firm throughout the swing. Then break or cock as the club passes the right hip.

On the downswing, the wrists remain cocked until the hands reach a point well below the hip.

Tony Lema's wrist action is wonderful to behold. He is able to bring the club head into the ball from an unbelievably late position. His wrists remain cocked until his hands are only a matter of inches short of the point from which they will deliver the club head.

When the uncocking of the wrists comes, the acceleration of the club head is tremendous. One source has computed that the club head whips through a 15-foot arc to catch up with the hands.

Keep your wrists cocked until the last possible moment. But certainly don't attempt to delay the action as Tony Lema does—not unless you have the great strength and superb coordination that Tony has.

After impact, the hands continue through the ball and on a line with the target. They finish high—another mark of the solid swing.

Throughout, of course, the swing is a smooth one. In summary, it's a "package deal" backswing; an even-tempered downswing, with the left side leading the hands through the ball, and, last, a high follow-through.

The Middle Irons

The middle irons—the 4, the 5, and the 6—demand much the same technique as the long irons. They are more versatile, offering a wide variety of shots. And you should be able to achieve a lot more accuracy with the middle or medium irons than with the long ones.

The backswing is shorter on the medium irons. How much shorter? That depends on your own swing.

Bobby Nichols, the 1964 P.G.A. Champion, is widely known for his mastery with the middle irons. His swing is a compact one and noticeably shorter than that of most other professionals. Yet he boasts a full shoulder turn. This gives him his distance. In addition, like Lema, he delays his wrist break until the last possible second.

Remember to strike the ball a descending blow, and hit the turf and the ball at the same time. Take a divot.

Uphill, downhill, and side-hill lies are played in much the same manner for irons as they are for woods. The downhill lie is played off the right heel. On an uphill lie, the ball is positioned off the left heel.

Take your time with side-hill lies; they're tricky. When the ball is above your feet, play a punch shot. Choke up on the club; cut down on the swing; play the ball off the right foot—punch it.

When the ball is below your feet, swing from the end of the club. Put your weight on your heels and bend your knees.

There is one last reason that the average player isn't as sharp on his irons as he should be. It's because he doesn't take the time that is necessary to select the proper club.

You can hit a perfect 5-iron shot, and wind up in nothing but trouble if the shot itself called for a 4. So know how to gauge distances and know your own capabilities with each club. A professional player will never choose a 5 iron for a shot without also considering the 4 and the 6. You should do the same.

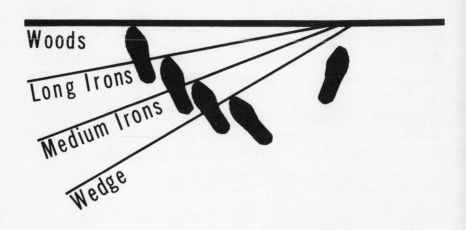

SIX

Pitching and Chipping

It was Gene Sarazen who invented the pitching wedge. And if you understand the physical principle that inspired the club and what he built into it, it may help you better to understand how it should be used.

It was the winter of 1931. Sarazen was in Florida, enjoying the sun and mulling over the tournament season just past. He signed up for a series of flying lessons, and one day he became intrigued by the action of the tail fin in causing the airplane to go up or down. Perhaps, he reasoned, a similar fin on a niblick (an 8 iron) would serve to put quick loft on a ball from the sand.

When a pilot wants to take off, he lowers the aircraft's tail fin. What Gene sought to do—and, in fact, did—was to produce a club whose face would come up as the sole went down.

A glaring weakness in Gene's game was his bunker play. It cost him strokes and victories in important tournaments. So Sarazen's finned-niblick theory offered him a chance to make a substantial improvement in his scoring ability. He tested the club diligently. When the season opened, it was ready. Traps were no more a problem. He won the British Open that year (1932) and soon after, the United States Open a second time. "I won both those championships with my wedge," Gene has said.

Today, of course, the wedge is used for much more than bunker play. The wide sole and deep loft the club offers make it useful any time you want to get the ball up into the air. It's no longer just the "sand iron," as Sarazen called it. Now a variation of it is known as the "pitching wedge."

As a stroke saver, the wedge is second only to the putter. Once you learn to be accurate with the club, it can be used to reclaim any shot that's missed between the tee and the green. Moreover, it's the wedge, more than any other club, that makes birdies from prospective pars, and eagles from birdies.

Often, in reporting the results of national tournaments, newspapers will testify that So-and-so's play was superior because he had a hot putter. His round included just 28 putts, the paper will exclaim. Yet often in these cases it's not the player's putting that is "hot," but his pitching. It is his wedge play that is getting him close to the cup, enabling him to get down in just one putt.

The wedge can be used with accuracy from a maximum distance of about 100 yards all the way down to within a yard or two of the green. Mostly, however, it is used in the 40- to 80-yard range. Watch the touring professionals. They will play the wedge (and the 9 iron, too) so as to pitch the ball two-thirds the distance to the hole and let it roll the other third. (On chip shots with the 6, and 7, or the 8, the opposite holds true; they plan to pitch the ball one-third the distance and let it roll the remaining two-thirds.)

Yet despite its importance and despite the fact that it is used more often than any other club except the putter, the wedge is mastered by only a relatively few amateur players.

The wedge shot has to be struck firmly and crisply and it is in this area that most players blunder. There is a tendency to hit the ball in a half-hearted way, to scoop the ball instead of really striking it. Such action will produce a blooped shot every time.

What you must do is let the club and its specialized construction work for you. Allow the club's broad flange to slide through the shot and the deep face to pop the ball into the air.

← *Golf, 1900. (The New York Public Library)*

> Use your normal grip, though you may want to choke up on the club just a bit. Play the ball about in the center, but more toward the right foot than the left.

> The wedge shot is all in the hands. There is little body action; the pivot is kept to a minimum. In fact, the weight must remain on the left foot throughout the shot. The stance is narrower than normal.

Watch Bobby Nichols execute a wedge shot. He brings the club head back slowly. There is a full wrist cock, even though the shaft of the club may be taken back to something less than a horizontal position.

On the downswing, the hands swing through. They lead the club head. They do not slap the ball. They do not push. They swing. Finish high with the hands.

No matter the distance of your pitch, your stroke should be basically the same. You control the distance of your shot by varying the amount of your backswing.

Invariably the pitch is a crucial shot, so there is an overwhelming desire on the part of the stroker to peek. Don't. As in every other shot, you must keep your head perfectly still.

One of the best "pitch men" on the tour is Tony Lema. In fact, in 1964, he was voted to *Golf Magazine*'s All-America Team for the way in which he demonstrated his mastery with the wedge.

Tony gets his hips into the ball more than most players. As he intiates the downswing, his left hip leads the action, moving laterally along the line of flight. This serves to "clear" his left hip so his right side can turn into the shot.

As his hips move forward, Tony straightens his left knee somewhat; his right knee breaks in toward the shot.

As on all of his irons, Tony's wedge stroke is characterized by a terrific wrist cock.

"How do the pros get so much backspin on the ball?" everyone asks. To most amateurs, nothing characterizes the pro player more than his ability to send a pitch shot skittering into reverse drive.

There is nothing mysterious about such a feat. It is done simply by emphasizing the instructional points outlined above. The club head does the work. It hits down and through the ball. It strikes cleanly, hitting the ball first and then the turf. If there is a "secret" to obtaining backspin on a pitch shot, it is one's ability to restrain himself and simply allow the flight of the ball to be dictated by the loft of the club.

Pitch and Run

The pitch and run in all of its myriad variations is the result of the inventiveness of the British. So claim historians of golf. In England and in Scotland, even in July and August, the winds whip in off the North Sea in near gale proportions. This is hardly a place for the high and graceful wedge shot.

Of course, the pitch and run has become popular in this country for reasons that have little to do with the weather. When you are at the edge of an expansive green, and the pin placement is to the rear of the green, meaning you have a lot of distance to cover, there is no shot more reliable than the crisp little pitch and run.

It is really startling how many amateur players disdain this shot, in

For the pitch and run, the pro player generally uses a 4 through a 7. (Shell's "Wonderful World of Golf")

spite of the fact that among professional players the pitch and run is universally accepted and used. Remember—there is no need to loft the ball high in the air, when you are close by the green. When you do, you sacrifice control and accuracy, and these two qualities are absolute musts in your short game.

For the pitch and run, the professional player uses almost any one of the middle irons, usually from a 4 through a 7 depending upon his lie and the distance he has to go.

The stance is taken with the feet a foot apart or less. It is a slightly open stance.

Your weight should be centered on your left side, and the ball played off the left heel.

Take the club straight back, away from the ball. The wrist break is just a slight one. The wrists must be kept firm throughout the shot.

As in the wedge shot, in the pitch and run distance is governed by the height of the backswing.

Throughout the shot the hands lead the club, and they must strike down and through the ball. Remember to hit the ball and the turf simultaneously. In this way you will get all the lift you need, and you will get some bite, too.

If you flub this shot a lot by skulling the ball, chances are that you are throwing the club head downward, and that there is no smoothness, no crisp action to your swing. Take your time on shots. Work to get meaningful rhythm into your swing. It is just as important here as when you are seeking to boom a drive 230 yards down a fairway.

Sam Snead says this shot is somewhat like a long putt, and so it is. You might be able to increase your success with the pitch and run swing if you look upon it as a kind of exaggerated putting stroke. And just as on a putt, use your ability to judge distance to determine how hard you should strike the ball.

Another key to success with this shot is proper planning. Both Palmer and Lema are masters in this department. Plan where you want the ball to land; pick out a precise target area. Generally, it is a good idea to map out your shot so that the ball "runs" about two-thirds the distance.

← *Nichols gets a good shoulder turn on this wedge shot. (Power Bilt Golf Clubs)*

The hands lead the club head. (Power Bilt Golf Clubs)

Aiming is part of the planning and one method of aiming is this: Imagine your target to be a circle, six feet in diameter. Aim for the centerpoint of the circle (a point which should be in a direct line with the cup). The closer you come to the center of the circle, the closer the ball will come to the hole. And if you get within the circle at all, and if your judgment of the distance is at all accurate, the ball will end up no more than three feet to either side of the pin.

There are a couple of other pieces of knowledge that will help you on the pitch and run. First, remember, if you have an uphill lie, play the ball more off your right foot. And, if you prefer to use a 6 iron from a level lie, use a 5 when the chip is uphill. This is because the incline adds loft.

Second and conversely, if the lie is a downhill one, use less club. Use a 7 or an 8, for example, from what would be a normal 6-iron lie.

The wedge shot is all hands; the pivot is held to a minimum. ("The Big Three," NBC–TV)

And play the ball off the left heel.

One factor that distinguishes the pros from the nonpros on the pitch and run is the amateur's tendency never to make the hole with his shot. Invariably his pitch falls short. Basically the reason for this is lack of confidence in one's swing. Confidence will come with practice; so train constantly in the pitch and run art.

Never underestimate the value of this shot. Because it is short and unspectacular, some players do. Never forget, you can fluff a drive, or flub a fairway iron, but the pitch and run can get you right back on the par course.

Most of your practice time should be spent in putting, but next to putting, pitching—short or long—is ranked second in importance. In this, to score well, you have to be proficient.

SEVEN

From Sand and Rough

"Julius Boros may appear completely harmless with his stoical and emotionless mannerism but he'll kill you on the golf course." So stated one of Boros' fellow touring competitors in discussing the talents of the forty-three-year-old veteran from Fairfield, Connecticut. It's true. To his opponents, Julius' clubs have come to have a lethal quality about them and his "deadliest weapon" of all is his sand wedge.

Early in 1964, *Golf Magazine* polled four hundred of the country's sports writers and sports broadcasters who regularly cover the game of golf, asking each to designate the professional golfer most proficient with each club of the eight principal clubs in the bag. Jack Nicklaus and Arnold Palmer monopolized the votes in the driver category, with Nicklaus finally winning out.

Balloting for the best player with the middle irons was even closer. Both Bobby Nichols and Ken Venturi showed almost equal strength. But in the voting for the best with the sand wedge, a trend started early and held, and when the final tabulation was completed it was almost a unanimous choice. The winner, of course, was Julius Boros.

No one plays all of his shots with perfect accuracy. Sometime or other during a round you are almost certain to send a shot into a

69

← *Golf, 1915. (The New York Public Library)*

bunker. But if you can, in the least way, develop some of the masterful hand action of Julius Boros in exploding from the sand, the traps need not hold the slightest terror for you.

Of course, it's not only the Boros system; the sand wedge itself helps to make the trap shot an easy one for you. If your clubs are handy, take a close look at the wedge. Notice its deep loft and its broad flange underneath. When the club is stroked properly, these two features combine to create a pancake cushion of sand beneath the ball. And it's this cushion of sand that serves to explode the ball from the bunker.

Don't be misled by players who pluck the ball from the sand with what seems to be an almost conventional chip shot. Always explode out—it's close to being an infallible method.

Remember, your first job is to get the ball out of the trap.

Plant the feet firmly in the trap. Wiggle them from side to side until you feel your stance is solid.

And spread your feet—"a little wider than for a normal short iron shot," Boros advises.

"Get over the ball," he says, "but don't crowd it. Avoid feeling cramped."

"The grip is the same as with any other iron," Boros states.

Aim to hit behind the ball—almost two inches behind it. Now bring the club head back, "crisply and without a drag." The club should be taken back slightly outside and across the ball.

"This shot," Boros says, "should be aimed slightly to the left of the target. This is to compensate for cutting across—but underneath—the ball."

"Take the club back no more than three-quarters of the normal distance and break the wrists early. Stroke firmly and follow through, digging a straight furrow as the club plows into the sand. Resist any rolling-over tendency in the hands and be sure to follow through."

Here the ball must be "clipped" cleanly from the hardpan. Bruce Devlin gets set to make the try. (CBS Golf Classic) →

The genius of Boros' wedge swing is in his hand action. (See photos, page 70.) At the address, the hands are slightly ahead of the club. Notice how the hands lead the club into the ball, and how the right hand turns over the shaft once the ball is struck.

Of course the stroke in the bunker has to be varied depending upon sand conditions. The description above is for normally soft sand. But if the sand is wet or hard-packed, you'll have to change your targeting spot. Instead of striking two inches in back of the ball, move closer—to about an inch behind it or even less. And you'll find that you'll be more successful with a 9 iron in hard-packed sand, or even with an 8.

Shorten your swing and your follow-through, too, even though you may have to power the stroke somewhat to get through the sand.

Balls buried in the sand, so as to be almost hidden from sight, are a special problem. In playing the plugged ball, remember to close the face of your wedge somewhat. This will give more exploding force to the club head. Play the ball off the left heel, and strike as much as three inches in back of the ball, so you'll be certain the club digs beneath it and "pops" it out.

One last bit of advice on playing shots like this. Set yourself for a more powerful swing, one that will carry smoothly and without hesitation through the deep sand.

Generally speaking, the longer the shot from the bunker, the less sand you take. But this theory works only to a point—up to approximately 25 or 35 yards, in fact. Beyond that, the explosion won't serve you very well.

On longer shots, you'll have to try to "pick" the ball from the bunker. Such shots are extremely difficult because the ball must be clipped cleanly without the club head digging into or even striking the sand. Be careful; it is easy for this shot to go awry, yet there is no other way.

What club to use? If it's a normal 6-iron shot, use it.

Address the ball in the same way you address a normal fairway shot, but in this there is only the slightest shifting of weight when the

← *A high follow-through characterizes the proper trap shot swing. ("The Big Three," NBC–TV)*

Boros spreads his feet, gets over the ball. He takes the club back about three-quarters of what would be a normal shot. The downswing is firm and well-controlled. The wrists break early. Throughout, the hands lead the action. Boros aims to hit behind the ball—about two inches behind it. (Wilson Sporting Goods)

Notice how Boros' right hand climbs over the shaft, but only well after the ball is struck. A good follow-through completes the stroke. (Wilson Sporting Goods)

swing is executed. It's all done with the wrists.

It's also hazardous to try to play a wood from the sand but, when you're unfortunate enough to catch a fairway bunker, you often have no other choice. Of course, don't try for a normal wood distance on a shot like this. Simply bring the club head around to meet the ball. Be satisfied with the distance you get.

Here again the hands and wrists have to do the work, and the weight shift is held to a minimum. Don't take any sand with the club. Simply skim it lightly into the ball; don't under any circumstances hit down on the ball.

Playing a wedge shot from sandy rough presents still another set of problems. Here, play the ball more off the right foot than in the more conventional trap shot. Use basically the same stroke; but take the club head back a bit higher, and when you come through, hit down on the ball.

The same stroke should be used when you're in deep grass. In this case, however, strike an inch or so in back of the ball. A cushion of grass will be formed between the club face and the ball, and serves to arc the ball out of the bunker.

While only half a dozen or so sand and rough shots are described here, there is an infinite variety of them, each tailored to a different lie and different distance. Each requires some type of variation in the wedge shot from the sand. This is your basic trouble shot. Follow Boros' advice: Get a firm stance; open the club face; hit behind the ball; swing through. Let the hands and wrists do the work.

Learn this one shot well. Develop confidence in your ability to execute it. Once this is gained, shots from the sand—in all their manifold variations—will offer you only the slightest bit of concern.

Ladies' Golf at Bideford Devon. (The New York Public Library)

EIGHT

Putting

Putting is the pay-off. No aspect of golf is as important.
→ If you don't agree, just look at the statistics of the art. On a course rated at par 72, thirty-six strokes—two putts a hole—are putting strokes. These figures imply that putting is 50 per cent of the game. It may not be quite that high but it is pretty close to that figure and so it is really the one department where you have an opportunity to save strokes.

It is putting more than anything else that distinguishes the score of the professional player from one who is not so professional. Take notice: there are no poor putters on the professional tour. Some players putt better than others, of course, but no one, not even the lowliest of the rabbits, is the least way inept in this department.

Again, look at the statistics. Most of the touring professionals *average* thirty putts a round, or slightly over that figure. This means that one-third of their greens are one-putt greens. That sounds sensational, and it is.

If you are shooting in the 80's, you are undoubtedly taking thirty-five to forty putts a round. And if you are shooting in the 90's, you are using forty putts a round. Obviously, then, if you are seeking to improve your score there is no better way than to improve your putting. (The next time you play a round of golf, keep a separate tally of your putting strokes; the number you accrue may surprise you.)

It is generally agreed that today Billy Casper, Arnold Palmer, and Gene Littler are the most consistent of the touring professionals on the putting green, and, furthermore, that they are endowed with some great and special talent that enables them to hole the ball in a manner that implies divine intervention. Casper, Palmer, and Littler are not so blessed; no one is. There is no trick, no special talent to it. Like long division or good penmanship, putting can be learned. To putt successfully is a matter of mastering the fundamentals of the putting grip, the stance, and the stroke. Of course, your mental attitude is important too. You have to boast an air of confidence.

Begin by selecting a putter that is suited for the course where you expect to do most of your playing. If the greens are fast, the light and responsive blade putter is probably best for you. Most of the pros use

The Billy Casper putting stance; it's all in the wrists, he says. (Wilson Sporting Goods)

a blade—with a flange. But if the greens are particularly slow, a mallet putter may be best.

You can buy putters today that are terribly bizarre, but don't. In its New York headquarters the U.S.G.A. exhibits one putter with four distance adjustments for angle and distance; another features a hollow chamber in the head where different-sized weights are to be inserted. Stay away from clubs like these; be conventional. And, incidentally, avoid the wood-shafted putter, too. These are charming, all right, but dampness and cold weather warp the wood and that's not so good.

In developing your own putting style, don't copy. Your style must be your own, although of course you can pick up individual bits and pieces of by watching professionals in action. For example, on the putting green Arnold Palmer uses a knock-kneed stance; he putts almost entirely with his hands. I don't believe there are many players who would be successful using Palmer's method. To most people it is awkward. Yet there are brief facets of Palmer's style—the way in which he locks his elbows into his sides, for instance—that can be incorporated into the system of putting you plan to develop for yourself.

In other words, your style must be completely your own. Your stance may be open; it may be more closed. You may putt from a crouch, or you may be more upright. You may stroke at the ball or, instead, you may jab at it. But no matter what characteristics of style you develop, once they are developed, stick to them.

Of Billy Casper, often hailed as the finest putter of the day, Ken Venturi says, "Casper's secret is his consistency, his ability to do the same thing over and over again in exactly the same way." So, too, you must have this aptitude for "stickability." Once you decide upon your style, give it a fair trial.

The Grip

The putting grip must be a firm one so as to allow you to have absolute control over the club. And it must also serve to mesh the hands into a single power-producing unit. Professional players achieve these two goals—control and unified action—by using what is termed the reverse overlap grip.

In his putting stance, Casper places his feet about a foot apart. His right foot is drawn back an inch or two from the line. Casper's arms move only slightly. It's

his wrists that do all the work. Notice how he accelerates the club head slightly on the forward swing. The ball is struck a descending blow so it overspins. (Wilson Sporting Goods)

Throughout the stroke, Casper keeps his head perfectly still. The Casper stroke is more of a jab than a smooth and easy stroke. (Wilson Sporting Goods)

In the reverse overlap style, the forefinger of the left hand rides over the last two fingers of the right hand. The thumbs point down the shaft. Try it; notice how the palms almost face one another, and how compact the grip is.

The left hand is in a strong position on the shaft, but with the forefinger of the left hand overlapping the fingers of the right, neither hand can dominate the other to the extent of producing an uneven and thereby inaccurate stroke.

Now, how firmly should the putter be held? The grip must be firm, yet it must be comfortable. Billy Casper advises how to achieve this balance: "I find this an easy problem to solve by imagining that the handle of the putter is a fresh egg. Squeeze the egg too hard and you'll break it; hold it too loosely and you'll drop it. Treat the putter with the same respect you would an egg."

Casper's main point is that the grip should be free of all tension. If tensed, the wrist and forearm are certain to act in such a way as to produce an inaccurate stroke.

Of course, not every professional uses the reverse overlap style. There are variations of every type. Some players interlock their fingers; some overlap the left hand over the right as in a wood shot. But generally these two methods produce power in the stroke; and in putting, power isn't needed.

California's Jerry Barber, when he plays, one of the surest putters on the tour, grips the club with his right hand turned to the right. In this way he can only hit the ball straight. Bob Rosburg uses his baseball grip.

The Stance

The putting stance is completely unlike any other you might use in a round of golf. It's more relaxed; there is no weight shift. And, as you prepare to stroke, you should be in a semi-crouch over the ball. The ball should be played from a position directly opposite the left heel. So Billy Casper advises. "The ball should be far enough out from the foot so that your forearms are just a fraction of an inch clear of your body," says Casper. "But don't play the ball so far out that you feel cramped.

"Your feet should be set about a foot apart," Casper advises. "The

Take your time making your survey; it pays. ("The Big Three," NBC–TV)

position of the right foot should be a matter of personal comfort, but I draw my right foot back about an inch or two behind the line. This is what is called a closed stance, and I feel it gives me a freer, firmer stroke.

"The center of your putter blade should be placed behind the ball, square to the putting line. You should bend forward at the waist, your weight on the balls of your feet, your knees slightly flexed. Your eyes should be directly above the blade, and your hands should be behind the ball, opposite the blade, with your forearms no more than lightly brushing your trousers."

In contrast to what Casper suggests in the way of a stance, some players concentrate their body weight entirely on the left foot, the right plays no part in the stroke at all. Jack Nicklaus has a unique style. His weight is back on his right foot when he shoots; his right shoulder very low.

What this means, of course, is that there is no accepted stance style. What you must do is experiment until you find the stance position that allows you to hit the ball firmly but comfortably.

The Stroke

"The secret of sound putting is the wrists," says Billy Casper. Casper, like the majority of players on the tour, is a wristy putter. "We rely on the wrists," Casper says, "because we know that the very highest degree of accuracy can be achieved only with the lowest degree of body movement. The fewer moving parts in your stroke, the straighter and more consistent your putts will be."

If you have an opportunity, watch Casper, whether you see him in person on the tour or on television. His wrist is a hinge. When he putts, Casper moves his arms only when absolutely necessary. On short putts his arms don't move at all. On medium-length putts they move almost imperceptibly. And on really long putts, where accuracy has to be sacrificed for sheer power, his right forearm swings back only about two or three inches, and this despite the fact that he raises the club on the backswing as much or more than anyone else on the tour.

Casper accelerates the club slightly in bringing it forward. (Note how the club head's increased speed has created a blur in Photo 5 of the sequence on page 91. Also notice that throughout the stroke Casper keeps the club head close to the ground.)

When you bring the club head forward and strike the ball, you must impart overspin to it, for overspin is what makes the ball hold the line. To do this, simply bring the club head forward so that it is positioned a few degrees from the perpendicular. This means the ball will be struck a descending blow and this will serve to overspin the ball. It's that easy.

The follow-through? Don't be concerned about it. Watch Casper's stroke. It finishes shortly after the ball is struck.

Another factor is all-important in putting: Throughout the stroke, the face of the putter must remain at right angles to the line of the stroke. Never break the face to the inside or the outside; from address to follow-through, the putter should be positioned precisely as it is to be at the instant the ball is struck.

And, as the whole world knows, when you putt, you must keep your head perfectly still.

If you follow Billy Casper's method of putting, you may feel you are tapping the ball more than stroking it. Well, you're right. The

Throughout the stroke, the face of the putter must remain at right angles to the line of the stroke. (Shell's "Wonderful World of Golf")

Casper style is really more of a jab than a smooth and easy-flowing stroke.

Most pros prefer to tap the ball—smoothly—into the cup, but there are a good number of strokers on the tour. Julius Boros is one; so is Art Wall. They sweep the ball toward the cup almost as if the putter were a broom. It is a more difficult style to master, and when the putt is a particularly long one, the sweep stroke presents serious problems.

Of course, one's ability with the putter is not determined by whether he is a tapper or a stroker. Putting, no matter the style, involves the admixture of the fundamentals of the grip, stance, and stroke plus a few other talents. And it's the "few others" that sometimes can be the deciding factor in holing a putt.

First of all, you have to be able to judge the distance the ball has to carry. Being accurate in this regard is much more a matter of experience than anything else. One thing you should always do, especially on long putts, is to walk off the distance from the ball to the hole. This is all-important. Not only does your reading help you to determine the amount of force you'll have to use in striking the ball, it serves to relax you somewhat after your charge down the fairway following that last iron shot.

Of course, the speed and direction of the ball on the putt are governed by other factors besides distance. Your reading also has to determine whatever undulations exist in the green's surface. Look over the green from at least two angles. And make note of the height of the grass, whether it is wet or dry (or neither), and its "grain"— the way in which the blades of grass are lying.

It's not difficult to tell which way the grain lies. Look toward the cup from a position in back of your ball. If the grass has a dull sheen to it, then you can be sure it's growing away from you. This means, of course, the ball when stroked will roll faster and for a longer distance than under ordinary conditions.

If the sheen is to your right as you survey, the grain is from right to left. Grain, incidentally, becomes an increasing important factor on greens that are not close-cut.

If you are putting on a course that's new to you, you should find

← *The stroke ends shortly after the ball is struck. (CBS Golf Classic)*

out what type of grass the greens are made of. The species can make an important difference. Sam Snead is reckoned an excellent putter on the Bermuda-carpeted greens of the southeastern United States. This is because he likes to bang his putts, and on Bermuda grass you can bang them. But on a close-clipped desert course like Las Vegas, where Bermuda is just an island in the Atlantic Ocean, Snead has his problems.

Distance, the height of the grass, its moisture content, its species, and so forth—there are a lot of factors that must be weighed before you strike the ball. So take your time on the green; it pays.

Downhill putts and uphill ones perplex even the best players. About all you can do on these is determine where the ball will break. Go for that spot and float the ball in from there.

Of these two, the downhill putt is considered the hardest. And if it is inclined to curl either to the right or left, it is particularly tough. Tighten your grip on these and all downhill putts, for this will serve to brake the ball.

On uphill putts, stroke for a point beyond the cup. This helps to overcome the common mistake of leaving the ball short of the hole.

The next time you're out on the course, pay particular attention to how you miss your putts. It's not a bad idea to chart your putts for an entire round. You'll get a clear idea of what habits—good or bad—you've developed.

The chances are that such a survey will reveal that you're missing the cup on the left-hand side. Up to 80 per cent of golfers do. The malady is particularly easy to notice on short putts—those that are 3 to 10 feet in length.

It's not hard to analyze why this happens. Most golfers give way to a tendency to turn the club face inboard at the instant the face of the blade strikes the ball. To overcome this, you must determine to keep the club face square to the putting line throughout the stroke. Don't let it waver one iota.

The tendency to strike to the left, like most other bad habits that beset you on the green, can be overcome by practice. To be a good putter, to develop the "touch" and the "feel" of the art, you must drill in the fundamentals of your stroke over and over again. It's estimated that the pros spend more time practicing their putting than all other phases of their game combined.

Billy Casper learned to putt as a youngster in San Diego; he would stay on the greens after dark practicing by the light from matches. It was this sort of determination that won him his outstanding putting touch.

Practice played an important part in Casper's victory in the U. S. Open Championship at Winged Foot Country Club in 1958. Billy experienced difficulty with his putting during his practice rounds. He worked for more than two hours to correct his problem. Finally he found the mistake and, after a tiny correction in his grip, sank a dozen practice putts in a row from 10 feet or better. He then went out and won the championship.

If you're not limited to just country club practice greens when you want to drill on the fundamentals of your grip, stance, and stroke, you can improve by putting on the living-room carpet. Just a few minutes a day can make a substantial difference in your stroking action.

Practice, by making you a better putter, will help to improve your confidence in yourself. And there is no aspect of the art of putting that is more important. If you are not already aware of the fact, any golf instructor will tell you that more putts are missed for mental reasons than for mechanical ones.

Take Arnold Palmer. His confidence, more than any other factor, is responsible for his brilliance on the greens. His belief that he can and will hole anything from 15 feet out has affected the style of play of dozens of young pros. Seldom do they lag for position close to the hole. It's custom now to go for the whole ball of wax. What's more, the system works.

On the greens, no one putts with more confidence than Billy Casper. Sam Snead, once practicing with Billy and watching him sink putts with calm assurance from every part of the green, told him, "Some day you're going to find out how hard those are and start missin' 'em."

Like Casper, *know* you are going to make the shot. Develop a positive mental attitude every time you mount the green. It's the first and most important act you can perform when it comes to getting the ball down.

Golf in the 1600's. (The New York Public Library)

NINE

The Rules

Think about it a minute and you will come to realize that the Rules of Golf are really quite simple ones. Even though they may have caused you difficulty in the past, and may again in the future, what you have to consider is that golf is a game of an infinite number of variations. These stem from the fact that no two courses are alike, playing conditions are seldom the same, any number of people up to four can play and competition can be of any number of types.

Despite these variations, and all of the others that these imply, the complete Rules of Golf, as approved by the United States Golf Association, are brief enough to be packaged up in a tidy little 94-page booklet. (You can purchase the booklet for 25 cents. Request it from the U.S.G.A., 40 East 38th St., New York, N.Y., 10016.)

At the outset, the Rules of Golf were meager ones. There were just 13 of them and it has taken all of 20 years for these to evolve to their present length and breadth. Now, every situation is covered.

The rules are easy to understand. And they are fair. As Executive Director of the U.S.G.A., Joseph C. Dey says, "The rules of golf are as much concerned with the rights of golf as the wrongs."

Of course, the infinite number of circumstances that golf presents means that rule interpretation is more important in golf than it is in most other sports. Many people, when they have a problem concerning the Rules, go right to the top. The U.S.G.A. receives inquiries every year from all sources; from golf associations, club officials and from just plain golfers. (According to the records of the organization, one out of every four inquiries is from a woman golfer, an indication that femme interest in the Rules, when related to the comparatively slight number of women in the total golfing population, greatly outstrips male concern. No one has deduced why.)

Rule inquiries to the U.S.G.A. are of all types. One letter-writer wanted to know, "Is it legal to tee off from the top of the tee marker?"

The U.S.G.A. offered no other comment on this unique play other than to state simply, "There is nothing to prohibit this because tee markers are within the teeing ground as defined in Definition 32." Despite the favorable ruling of the U.S.G.A. on this point, the strategy has not become widespread.

Some questions hint a problem far beyond the world of golf. Said one inquirer, "Is there any ruling that a husband and a wife must play together as a team in an amateur Scotch foursome?" Hesitatingly the U.S.G.A. fielded this one.

A professional player wrote to ask if it would be "legal to wear an apparatus on the left shoe with an arrow pointing in the direction you want to putt on the putting surface. This is attached to the shoe and does not touch the ground."

The U.S.G.A. asked for a sample but none was sent.

In one recent year, the U.S.G.A. tabulated all of the rule inquiries received and determined the rules most-questioned was Rule 35, "The Putting Green." Some of the difficulties that players might encounter are mentioned in succeeding paragraphs.

Can the player touch the line of putt? "No," say the rules, but there are two exceptions.

A player may pick up or otherwise remove any loose impediment from the line of putt. And the player is also allowed to repair any ball marks that lie on the line.

A ball lying on the putting green can be lifted and cleaned without the player incurring any penalty, declares Rule 35.

Is your caddie allowed to point out to you the direction in which your putt may break? Of course he is, say the rules. But he is not allowed to touch the putting line at all when giving you your directions.

Can you place a coin on the green to help you sight your putting line? The rules say "No" to this one.

Likewise it's a breach of the regulations to roll a ball on the green or scrape the green's surface in order to determine the condition of the putting surface.

Most everyone knows how to mark a ball on the putting green, but the rule covering this is worth repeating. Place the marker "immediately behind" the ball states the rulebook.

If the marker is in someone else's line of putt, move it to one side. This rule suggests you move the marker the distance of one or more head-lengths of your putter.

What is the penalty should a player putt out of turn? If you should be guilty of this breach, your opponent can make you replay the shot.

Is there a penalty if your ball strikes your opponent's ball on the putting green? There is, indeed—if both balls are within sixty feet of the hole. The penalty is an awesome two strokes. After the errant shot, you must play your ball from where it lies.

Rule 29 is another one with which golfers have their troubles. This rule is titled, "Ball Lost, Out of Bounds or Unplayable."

Golfers know that should they lose a ball by virtue of an out-of-bounds shot, then the next stroke is to be played from a point as near as possible to the spot where the original ball was played. Of course, a penalty stroke is incurred.

What if the original stroke was a drive played from the tee? In replaying the shot, does the player have to re-tee at the same spot where the ball was teed originally? "No," say the rules; the ball may be teed anywhere in the teeing area.

May a player stand out-of-bounds to play a ball that lies within bounds. "Yes, indeed he may," the rules state.

What is the ruling should you and your opponent argue over whether your ball is playable or not. You say it's not playable; he says it is. Who's right?

You are; the rule book deems you the "sole judge" as to whether your ball is playable or not. You can declare your ball to be unplayable anywhere on the course.

Of course, once you declare your ball unplayable, you incur the penalties that such a declaration implies. For instance, you may suffer the "stroke and distance" penalty described above.

Or let's say the ball is lying close by a rock. In order to be able to play the ball, it has to be moved. After declaring the ball unplayable, you must drop the ball behind the point where it originally rested. Of course, here again a penalty stroke is exacted.

Many players are unsure about the provisional ball rule. This is the U.S.G.A.'s Rule 30, but actually it is a carry-over from Rule 29.

A provisional ball is one played when your original ball is deemed lost (except when it is lost in a water hazard).

You must announce to your playing opponent your intention to play a provisional ball. And such a ball has to be played *before* you launch your search for the original ball. This section of the rule is often violated.

If, as you move down the course, you do find your original ball, the provisional ball, to quote the U.S.G.A., "may be abandoned."

Rule 33 is a third rule about which golfers often query the U.S.G.A. This rule concerns "Hazards and Water Hazards."

Though some may be reluctant to admit it, most golfers fully realize that when a ball lies in or touches any type of hazard, nothing can be done to improve the lie of the ball. Nor, as in the case of a trap, can you touch or smooth the sand to improve the ball's position.

When in a trap, some golfers take a practice shot at an imaginary ball, swatting the sand with their club as they do. This is helpful in determining the condition of the sand—but it is illegal. The penalty is two strokes.

However, there are a number of ways you can help yourself when trapped without incurring penalty strokes. You can plant your feet firmly into the sand. You can remove any obstructions that impede your stroke (such as the groundkeeper's rake). If your ball is completely buried in the sand (or amidst leaves in the woods), you can clean away enough sand (or leaves) so the top of the ball is revealed.

In removing leaves and twigs to uncover a ball, what is the ruling should the ball roll? There rules are fair; there is no penalty. All you must do is replace the ball to where it lay originally.

When your ball tumbles into a pond or similar water hazard, how far behind the hazard must you play the next ball. The rules say you can get as far behind the hazard as you want. Just remember to keep on a line between the tee and the point where the ball crossed into the water. The penalty in this situation is one stroke.

It is significant that Section One of the Rules of Golf is devoted to "Etiquette." Manners are a golfing must and the U.S.G.A. is quick to recognize this fact.

Of the rules of etiquette, the very first one is the one most often breached. It declares that you should never "move, talk or stand" close to another player while he is addressing the ball or stroking it.

Many players are strict with themselves about obeying the rules of golf. But the problem is they don't know the rules; at least they don't know all of them.

Study the rule book. And do as many golfers do, keep a copy handy in your golf bag.

Appendix

JULIUS BOROS

PERSONAL STATISTICS
   Date of birth: March 3, 1920
   City: Fairfield, Conn.
   Height: 5 ft. 11½ in. Weight. 200 lb.
   Golf professional since: Dec. 15, 1949
   Club: Mid-Pines N.C. C.C.
   Lowest competitive score: 64
      1958 Hot Springs, Ark. Open
   Lowest 72-hole score: 268
      1952 Texas Open, Brackenridge, Tex. G.C.

CAREER HIGHLIGHTS
   Winner, National Open, 1952, 1963
   Twice winner, World Championship, 1952, 1955
   Twice Leading Money Winner, 1952, 1955
   Winner, P.G.A. Golfer of the Year, 1952, 1963
   Member Ryder Cup Team, 1959, 1963
   Winner, Colonial Invit., 1960, 1963
   Winner, Buick Open, 1963
   Member, Golf Advisory Staff, Wilson Sporting Goods.

BILLY CASPER

PERSONAL STATISTICS
    Date of birth: June 24, 1931
    City: San Diego, Calif.
    Height: 5 ft. 11 in. Weight: 210 lb.
    Golf professional since: April, 1954
    Club: Apple Valley C. C., Apple Valley, Calif.
    Lowest competitive score: 64
       1956 Dallas Open, Preson Hollow Texas C.
    Lowest 72-hole score: 267
       1958 Miller Open, Tripoli, C. C.

CAREER HIGHLIGHTS
    Winner, Labatts Open, 1956
    Winner, Phoenix Open, 1957
    Winner, Bing Crosby Inv., 1958, 1963
    Winner, New Orleans Open, 1958
    Winner, Buick Open, 1958
    Runner-up PGA Championship, 1958
    Second money winner, $14,323.75, 1958
    Winner, U.S. Open, 1958
    Winner, Portland Open, 1959, 1960, 1961
    Winner, Insurance City Open, 1963
    Winner, Vardon Trophy, 1960, 1963
    Winner, Palm Springs Desert Classic, 1965
    Member, Golf Advisory Staff, Wilson Sporting Goods.

BILLY MAXWELL

PERSONAL STATISTICS
Date of birth: July 23, 1929
City: Abilene, Texas
Height: 5 ft. 7½ in. Weight: 160 lb.
Golf professional since: Feb. 1954
Club: El Camino C. C., Oceanside, Calif.
Lowest competitive score: 63
Big Spring, Texas C. C.
Lowest 72-hole score: 264
    1956 Mexican Open, Chapultepec C.

CAREER HIGHLIGHTS
Winner, National Amateur, 1951
Winner, Azalea Open, 1955
Winner, Mexican Open, 1956
Winner, Memphis Open, 1958
Winner, Palm Springs Classic, 1961
Winner, Insurance City Open, 1961
Winner, Puerto Rico Open, 1961
Winner, Dallas Open, 1962
Member of Ryder Cup Team, 1963
Member, Golf Advisory Staff, Wilson Sporting Goods.

SAM SNEAD

PERSONAL STATISTICS
    Date of birth: May 27, 1912
    City: Hot Springs, Va.
    Height: 5 ft. 11 in. Weight: 182 lb.
    Golf professional since: 1934
    Club: Greenbrier C. C., White Sulphur Springs, W. Va.
    Lowest competitive score: 59
    Sam Snead Festival, White Sulphur Springs, W. Va. G.C.
    Lowest 72-hole score: 263
        1951 Greenbrier Open, White Sulphur Springs, W. Va. G.C.

CAREER HIGHLIGHTS
    Winner, British Open, 1946
    Three-time winner, PGA Championship, 1942, 1949, 1951
    Three-time winner, Masters, 1949, 1952, 1954
    Three-time Leading Money Winner, 1938, 1949, 1950
    Four-time winner, Vardon Trophy, 1938, 1949, 1950, 1955
    Seven-time member of Ryder Cup Team, 1937, 1947, 1949, 1951,
        1953, 1955, 1959
    Three-time runner-up, U.S. Open, 1937, 1947, 1953
    Runner-up, Masters, 1957
    Member, Golf Hall of Fame
    Member, Golf Advisory Staff, Wilson Sporting Goods.

Index